piano • vocal • guitar

TOPCOUNTRYHITS
'04·'05

ISBN 0-634-09547-1

HAL•LEONARD®
CORPORATION
7777 W. BLUEMOUND RD. P.O. BOX 13819 MILWAUKEE, WI 53213

Visit Hal Leonard Online at
www.halleonard.com

CONTENTS

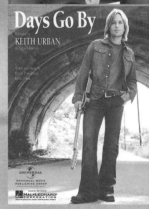

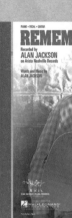

AMERICAN SOLDIER

Words and Music by TOBY KEITH
and CHUCK CANNON

In a steady four

I'm just try'n' to be a fa - ther, raise a daugh-ter and _ a son. _ Be a
do it for the mon - ey, there's _ bills that I _ can't pay. _ I don't

lov - er to _ their moth - er, ev - 'ry - thing to ev - 'ry - one. _ Up and
do it for _ the glo - ry, I just do it an - y - way. _ Pro -

at 'em bright _ and ear - ly, I'm all bus - 'ness in _ my suit. _ Yeah, I'm
vid - ing for _ our fu - ture's my re - spon - si - bil - i - ty. _ Yeah, I'm

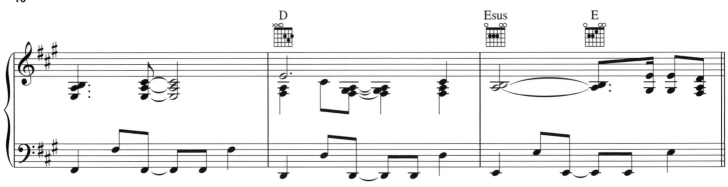

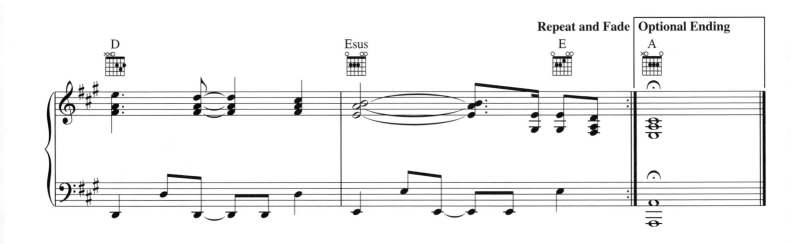

AWFUL, BEAUTIFUL LIFE

Words and Music by DARRYL WORLEY
and HARLEY ALLEN

Moderately fast

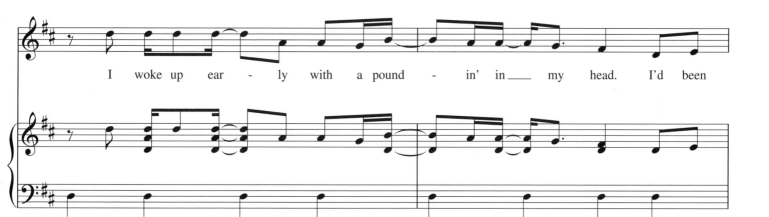

I woke up ear-ly with a pound-in' in __ my head. I'd been

out the night __ be-fore __ with all __ my friends.

14

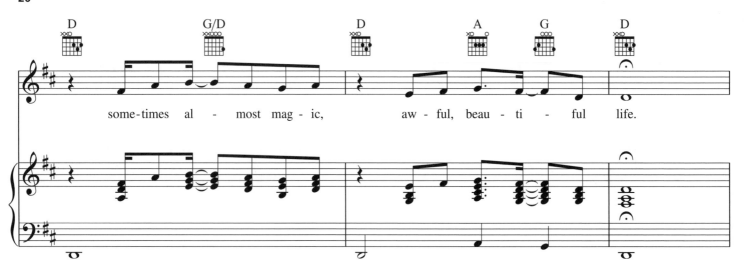

some-times al - most mag - ic, aw - ful, beau - ti - ful life.

A tempo

BACK WHEN

Words and Music by STAN LYNCH,
STEPHONY SMITH and JEFF STEVENS

Don't you re-mem-ber the fizz in the Pep-
I love my rec-ords, black and shin-y vi-

- per, pea-nuts in a bot-tle at ten, two and
- nyl, clicks and pops and white noise, man, they sound-ed

24

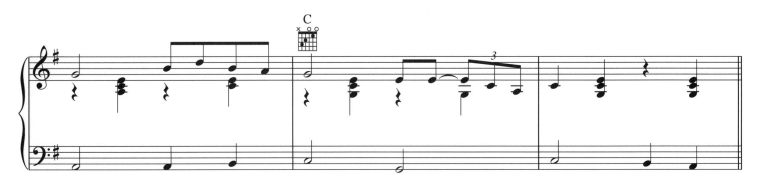

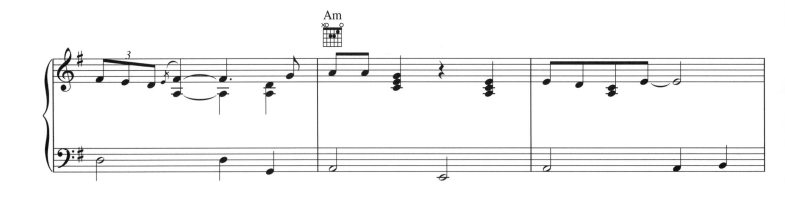

DAYS GO BY

Words and Music by MONTY POWELL
and KEITH URBAN

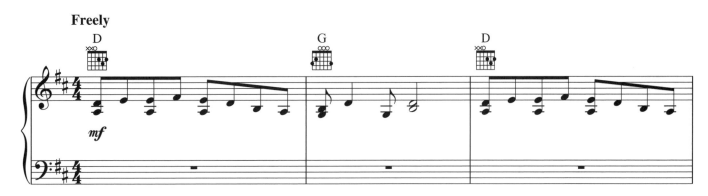

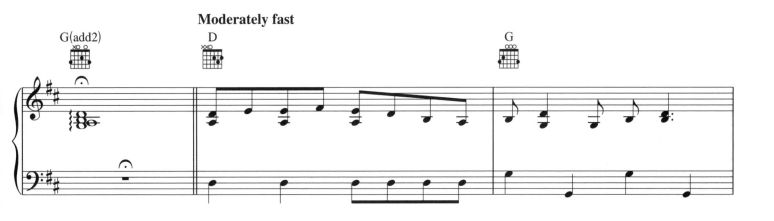

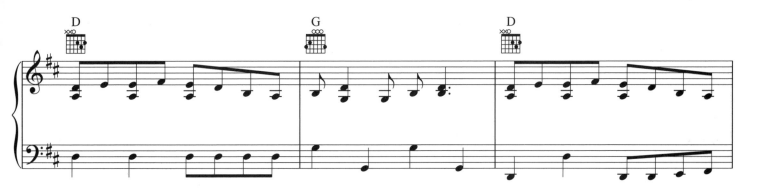

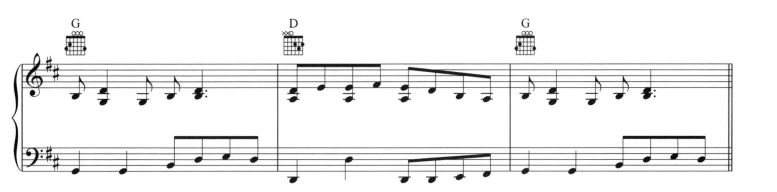

HOW AM I DOIN'

Words and Music by DIERKS BENTLEY
and WRITER X

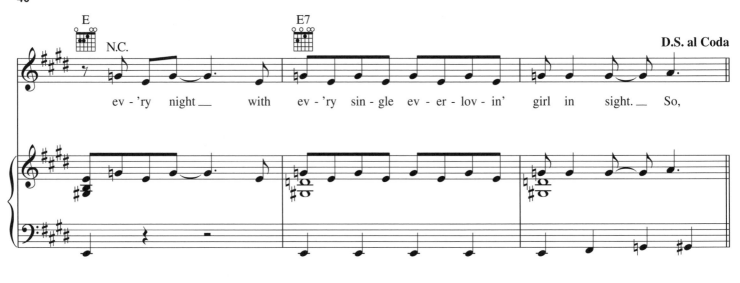

So,

ev - 'ry night ___ with ev - 'ry sin - gle ev - er - lov - in' girl in sight. ___ So,

Instrumental solo

IN A REAL LOVE

Words and Music by PHIL VASSAR
and CRAIG WISEMAN

Well, I was eight - een mak - in' min - i - mum wage, __ with a
I was twen - ty - two, work - in' dou - ble o - ver - time, I was

LONG BLACK TRAIN

Words and Music by
JOSH TURNER

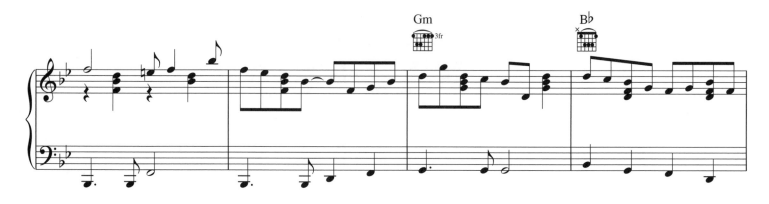

D.S. al Coda

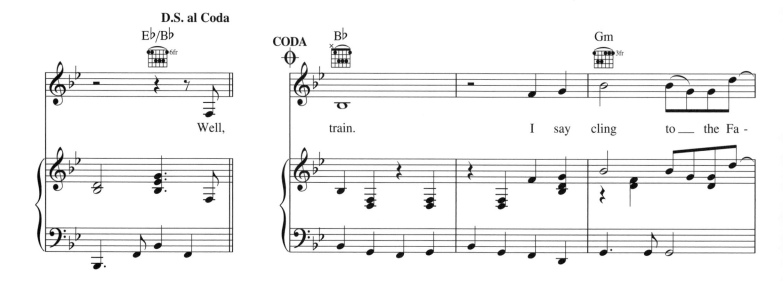

Well, train. I say cling to ___ the Fa -

ME AND YOU

Words and Music by SKIP EWING
and RAY HERNDON

Ev - 'ry day I live,____ try my best to give____ all I have to you.
Instrumental solo
Or - di - nar - y? No,____ real - ly don't think so.____ Just a pre - cious few____

To Coda ⊕

Thank the stars a - bove____ that we share this love,____ me and you.
ev - er make it last,____ get as luck - y as____

Instrumental ends

D.S. al Coda

CODA ⊕

____ me and you.

a tempo

rit.

Me and you.____

MR. MOM

Words and Music by RICHIE McDONALD,
RONALD HARBIN and DON PFRIMMER

Lost my job, came __ home mad, __ got a hug and a kiss and "that's __
Foot - ball, soc - cer and __ bal - let __ and squeeze in __ scouts and P. __

Mom.

Be -

fore I fall in bed to-night,__ if the dog did-n't eat the clas-

MUD ON THE TIRES

Words and Music by BRAD PAISLEY
and CHRIS DUBOIS

NOTHIN' TO LOSE

Words and Music by KEVIN SAVIGAR
and MARCEL CHAGNON

NOTHIN' 'BOUT LOVE MAKES SENSE

Words and Music by JOEL FEENEY,
GARY BURR and KYLIE SACKLEY

PARTY FOR TWO

Words and Music by SHANIA TWAIN
and R.J. LANGE

*Recorded a half step lower.

REDNECK WOMAN

Words and Music by GRETCHEN WILSON
and JOHN RICH

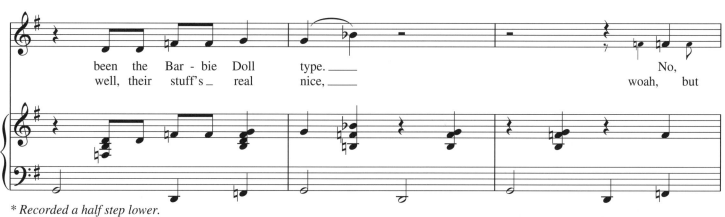

* *Recorded a half step lower.*

yeah.____ (Hell,   yeah!)

Instrumental solo

I'm a red - neck wom - an, I ain't no

REMEMBER WHEN

Words and Music by
ALAN JACKSON

Re-mem - ber when _____

the

we

ROUGH & READY

Words and Music by BLAIR MACKICHAN,
BRIAN WHITE and CRAIG WISEMAN

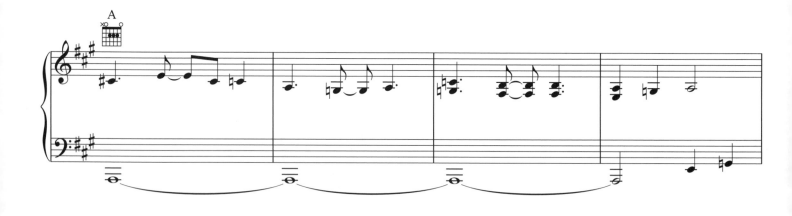

rough and read - y, ba - by.

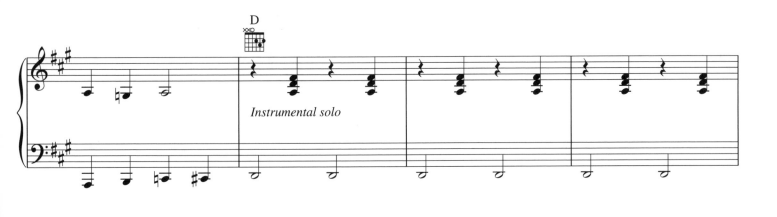

D

Instrumental solo

A

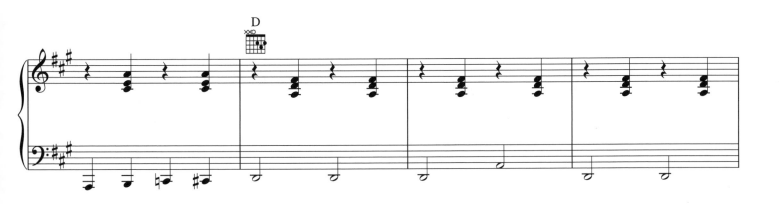

D

rough and read - y, _____

rough and read - y,   ba - by.

Repeat and Fade

Optional Ending

STAYS IN MEXICO

Words and Music by
TOBY KEITH

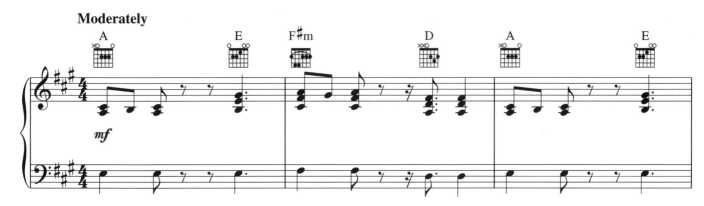

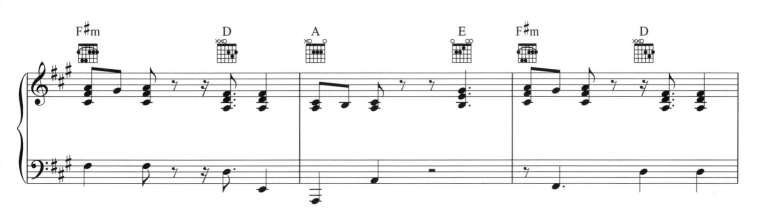

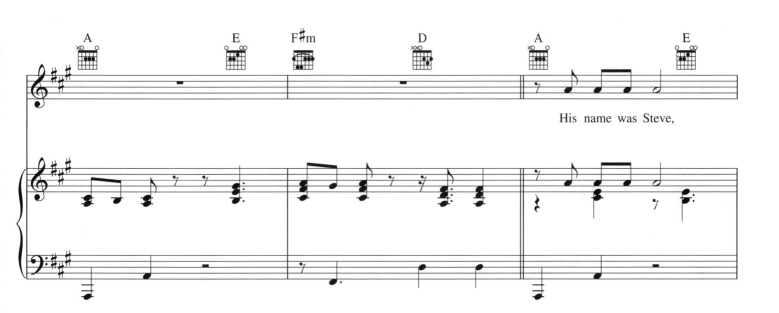

His name was Steve,

Phoe - nix, Ar - i - zo - na.

They start - ed danc - ing and it got real hot. Then it spilled o - ver to the

park - ing lot. One more te - qui - la, they were

fall - ing in love. One more's nev - er e - nough.

THAT'S WHAT IT'S ALL ABOUT

Words and Music by STEVE McEWAN
and CRAIG WISEMAN

work and you slave and you spend all day in your thank-less job. Then you
won't go to bed and ___ do what you said or eat their food. They

THE WOMAN WITH YOU

Words and Music by DAVID RAY FRASIER
and CRAIG WISEMAN

She hit the door, __ six - fif - ty - five, __ sack full of gro - ceries

girl I __ was __ with the busi - ness de - gree __ prob - 'ly would - n't

THIS ONE'S FOR THE GIRLS

Words and Music by AIMEE MAYO,
HILLARY LINDSEY and CHRIS LINDSEY

COUNTRY MUSIC HALL OF FAME

SONGBOOK SERIES

The Country Music Hall of Fame was founded in 1961 by the Country Music Association (CMA). Each year, new members are elected – and these books are the first to represent all of its members with photos, biographies and music selections related to each individual.

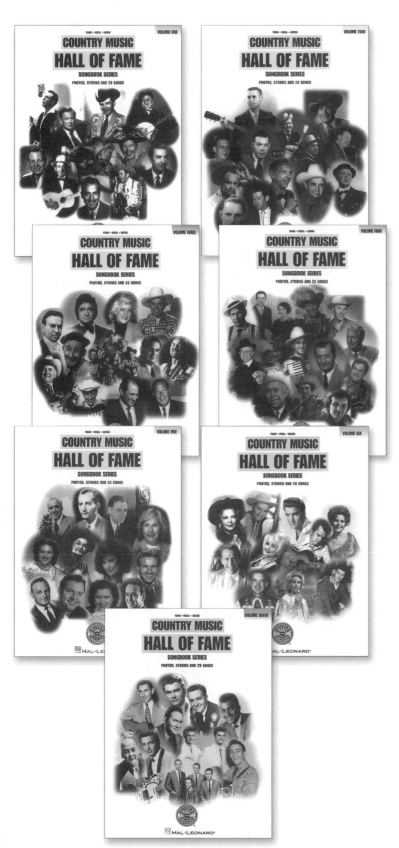

VOLUME 1
Features Jimmie Davis, Tennessee Ernie Ford, Minnie Pearl, Jim Reeves, Hank Williams, and others. Includes photos, stories, and 29 songs, including: The Ballad of Davy Crockett • Can the Circle Be Unbroken • Deep in the Heart of Texas • Jambalaya (On the Bayou) • May the Bird of Paradise Fly Up Your Nose • Mule Train • Rocky Top • You Are My Sunshine • Your Cheatin' Heart • and more.
_____00313058 P/V/G...$12.95

VOLUME 2
Features Roy Acuff, Owen Bradley, Lester Flatt and Earl Scruggs, Tex Ritter, Merle Travis, Bob Wills, and more. 29 songs, including: Divorce Me C.O.D. • He Stopped Loving Her Today • I'm Sorry • San Antonio Rose • Sixteen Tons • Wabash Cannon Ball • and more.
_____00313059 P/V/G...$12.95

VOLUME 3
Features Gene Autry, Johnny Cash, Roy Horton, Bill Monroe, Willie Nelson, Frances Preston, Ernest Tubb, and other Hall of Famers. 33 songs, including: Always on My Mind • Folsom Prison Blues • (I Never Promised You A) Rose Garden • It Makes No Difference Now • Kentucky Waltz • On the Road Again • Ring of Fire • Sugarfoot Rag • Tennessee Saturday Night • Tumbling Tumbleweeds • Walking the Floor Over You • and more.
_____00313060 P/V/G...$12.95

VOLUME 4
Features Eddy Arnold, Chet Atkins, the Original Carter Family, Merle Haggard, Pee Wee King, Hubert Long, Roger Miller, Floyd Tillman, and more. 32 songs, including: Bouquet of Roses • Dang Me • Green Green Grass of Home • Happy Trails • Heartbreak Hotel • If You've Got the Money (I've Got the Time) • John Henry • King of the Road • Mama Tried • Okie From Muskogee • Tennessee Waltz • Yakety Axe • and more.
_____00313061 P/V/G...$12.95

VOLUME 5
Features Patsy Cline, Jim Denny, Connie B. Gay, Loretta Lynn, Marty Robbins, and others. 32 songs, including: Blue Eyes Crying in the Rain • Coal Miner's Daughter • Crazy • 'Deed I Do • El Paso • I Fall to Pieces • The Long Black Veil • Pistol Packin' Mama • Ruby, Don't Take Your Love to Town • You Ain't Woman Enough • and more.
_____00313062 P/V/G...$12.95

VOLUME 6
PHOTOS, STORIES AND 28 SONGS
A wonderful treasury of country music legends, complete with photos and bios of each of the featured honorees. This volume showcases Hall of Fame inductees Johnny Bond, Harlan Howard, Brenda Lee, Buck Owens, Dolly Parton, Elvis Presley, Ray Price, Conway Twitty, Cindy Walker and Tammy Wynette. Includes photos, bios, and 28 songs from the artists: Above and Beyond • Act Naturally • Coat of Many Colors • D-I-V-O-R-C-E • Don't Be Cruel (To a Heart That's True) • Heartaches by the Number • Heartbreak Hotel • Hello Darlin' • Hot Rod Lincoln • I Will Always Love You • I'm Sorry • I've Got a Tiger by the Tail • It's Only Make Believe • Love Me Tender • Release Me • Stand by Your Man • Tomorrow Never Comes • You Don't Know Me • and more.
_____00313202 P/V/G...$12.95

VOLUME 7
PHOTOS, STORIES AND 28 SONGS
This volume features Country Music Hall of Fame honorees Bill Anderson, The Everly Brothers, Don Gibson, Waylon Jennings, The Jordanaires, Don Law, Sam Phillips, Webb Pierce, Charlie Pride and Faron Young. Includes photos and bios of each, plus 28 great representative songs: All I Have to Offer You Is Me • Ballad of a Teenage Queen • Battle of New Orleans • Big Bad John • Blue Suede Shoes • Bye Bye Love • Cathy's Clown • The Gambler • A Good Hearted Woman • Great Balls of Fire • Hello Walls • Hey Joe • I Can't Stop Loving You • Is Anybody Going to San Antone • Kiss an Angel Good Mornin' • Mammas Don't Let Your Babies Grow Up to Be Cowboys • Oh, Lonesome Me • Waterloo • When Will I Be Loved • and more.
_____00313203 P/V/G...$12.95

FOR MORE INFORMATION, SEE YOUR LOCAL MUSIC DEALER,
OR WRITE TO:

HAL•LEONARD®
CORPORATION
7777 W. BLUEMOUND RD. P.O. BOX 13819 MILWAUKEE, WI 53213

Visit Hal Leonard Online at
www.halleonard.com

Prices, contents and availability subject to change without notice.

The Ultimate Songbooks!

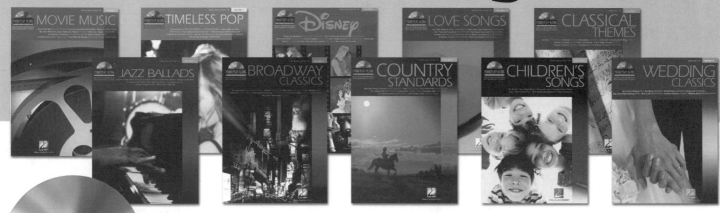

PIANO PLAY-ALONG

These great book/CD packs come with our standard arrangements for piano and voice with guitar chord frames plus a CD. The CD includes a full performance of each song as well as a second track without the piano part so you can play "lead" with the band.

VOLUME 1
MOVIE MUSIC

Come What May • Forrest Gump – Main Title (Feather Theme) • My Heart Will Go On (Love Theme from 'Titanic') • The Rainbow Connection • Tears in Heaven • A Time for Us • Up Where We Belong • Where Do I Begin (Love Theme).
00311072 P/V/G.........................$12.95

VOLUME 2
JAZZ BALLADS

Autumn in New York • Do You Know What It Means to Miss New Orleans • Georgia on My Mind • In a Sentimental Mood • More Than You Know • The Nearness of You • The Very Thought of You • When Sunny Gets Blue.
00311073 P/V/G.........................$12.95

VOLUME 3
TIMELESS POP

Ebony and Ivory • Every Breath You Take • From a Distance • I Write the Songs • In My Room • Let It Be • Oh, Pretty Woman • We've Only Just Begun.
00311074 P/V/G.........................$12.95

VOLUME 4
BROADWAY CLASSICS

Ain't Misbehavin' • Cabaret • If I Were a Bell • Memory • Oklahoma • Some Enchanted Evening • The Sound of Music • You'll Never Walk Alone.
00311075 P/V/G $12.95

VOLUME 5
DISNEY

Beauty and the Beast • Can You Feel the Love Tonight • Colors of the Wind • Go the Distance • Look Through My Eyes • A Whole New World • You'll Be in My Heart • You've Got a Friend in Me.
00311076 P/V/G.........................$12.95

VOLUME 6
COUNTRY STANDARDS

Blue Eyes Crying in the Rain • Crazy • King of the Road • Oh, Lonesome Me • Ring of Fire • Tennessee Waltz • You Are My Sunshine • Your Cheatin' Heart.
00311077 P/V/G $12.95

VOLUME 7
LOVE SONGS

Can't Help Falling in Love • (They Long to Be) Close to You • Here, There and Everywhere • How Deep Is Your Love • I Honestly Love You • Maybe I'm Amazed • Wonderful Tonight • You Are So Beautiful.
00311078 P/V/G.........................$12.95

VOLUME 8
CLASSICAL THEMES

Can Can • Habanera • Humoresque • In the Hall of the Mountain King • Minuet in G Major • Piano Concerto No. 21 in C Major ("Elvira Madigan"), Second Movement Excerpt • Prelude in E Minor, Op. 28, No. 4 • Symphony No. 5 in C Minor, First Movement Excerpt.
00311079 Piano Solo $12.95

VOLUME 9
CHILDREN'S SONGS

Do-Re-Mi • It's a Small World • Linus and Lucy • Sesame Street Theme • Sing • Winnie the Pooh • Won't You Be My Neighbor? (It's a Beautiful Day in This Neigh-borhood) • Yellow Submarine.
0311080 P/V/G $12.95

VOLUME 10
WEDDING CLASSICS

Air on the G String • Ave Maria • Bridal Chorus • Canon in D • Jesu, Joy of Man's Desiring • Ode to Joy • Trumpet Voluntary • Wedding March.
00311081 Piano Solo..................$12.95

VOLUME 11
WEDDING FAVORITES

All I Ask of You • Don't Know Much • Endless Love • Grow Old with Me • In My Life • Longer • Wedding Processional • You and I.
00311097 P/V/G $12.95

VOLUME 12
CHRISTMAS FAVORITES

Blue Christmas • The Christmas Song (Chestnuts Roasting on an Open Fire) • Do You Hear What I Hear • Here Comes Santa Claus (Right down Santa Claus Lane) • I Saw Mommy Kissing Santa Claus • Let It Snow! Let It Snow! Let It Snow! • Merry Christmas, Darling • Silver Bells.
00311137 P/V/G $12.95

VOLUME 13
YULETIDE FAVORITES

Angels We Have Heard on High • Away in a Manger • Deck the Hall • The First Noel • Go, Tell It on the Mountain • Jingle Bells • Joy to the World • O Little Town of Bethlehem.
00311138 P/V/G.........................$12.95

VOLUME 14
POP BALLADS

Have I Told You Lately • I'll Be There for You • It's All Coming Back to Me Now • Looks Like We Made It • Rainy Days and Mondays • Say You, Say Me • She's Got a Way • Your Song.
00311145 P/V/G $12.95

VOLUME 15
FAVORITE STANDARDS

Call Me • The Girl from Ipanema (Garota De Ipanema) • Moon River • My Way • Satin Doll • Smoke Gets in Your Eyes • Strangers in the Night • The Way You Look Tonight.
00311146 P/V/G $12.95

VOLUME 16
TV CLASSICS

The Brady Bunch • Green Acres Theme • Happy Days • Johnny's Theme • Love Boat Theme • Mister Ed • The Munsters Theme • Where Everybody Knows Your Name.
00311147 P/V/G $12.95

VOLUME 17
MOVIE FAVORITES

Back to the Future • Theme from E.T. (The Extra-Terrestrial) • Footloose • For All We Know • Somewhere in Time • Somewhere Out There • Theme from "Terms of Endearment" • You Light Up My Life.
00311148 P/V/G.........................$12.95

VOLUME 18
JAZZ STANDARDS

All the Things You Are • Bluesette • Easy Living • I'll Remember April • Isn't It Romantic? • Stella by Starlight • Tangerine • Yesterdays.
00311149 P/V/G.........................$12.95

VOLUME 19
CONTEMPORARY HITS

Beautiful • Calling All Angels • Don't Know Why • If I Ain't Got You • 100 Years • This Love • A Thousand Miles • You Raise Me Up.
00311162 P/V/G.........................$12.95

VOLUME 20
R&B BALLADS

After the Love Has Gone • All in Love Is Fair • I'll Be There • Let's Stay Together • Midnight Train to Georgia • Say You, Say Me • Tell It like It Is • Three Times a Lady.
00311163 P/V/G.........................$12.95

Prices, contents and availability subject to change without notice.

FOR MORE INFORMATION, SEE YOUR LOCAL MUSIC DEALER, OR WRITE TO:

HAL•LEONARD® CORPORATION

7777 W. BLUEMOUND RD. P.O. BOX 13819 MILWAUKEE, WI 53213

Visit Hal Leonard Online at **www.halleonard.com**

0704

Contemporary & Classic Country

More great country hits from Hal Leonard arranged for piano and voice with guitar chords.

#1 Country Hits of the Nineties – 2nd Edition

The second edition of this great compilation includes 26 hits: Achy Breaky Heart • Boot Scootin' Boogie • Chattahoochee • Check Yes or No • Friend in Low Places • Longneck Bottle • Love Without End, Amen • My Maria • She Is His Only Need • Wide Open Spaces • You're Still the One • more.

00311699......................$12.95

51 Country Standards

A collection of 51 of country's biggest hits, including: (Hey Won't You Play) Another Somebody Done Somebody Wrong Song • By the Time I Get to Phoenix • Could I Have This Dance • Daddy Sang Bass • Forever and Ever, Amen • God Bless the U.S.A. • Green Green Grass of Home • Islands in the Stream • King of the Road • Little Green Apples • Lucille • Mammas Don't Let Your Babies Grow Up to Be Cowboys • Ruby Don't Take Your Love to Town • Stand by Me • Through the Years • Your Cheatin' Heart.

00359517......................$14.95

100 Most Wanted

Highlights: A Boy Named Sue • Break It to Me Gently • Crying My Heart out over You • Heartbroke • I.O.U. • I Know a Heartache When I See One • Mammas Don't Let Your Babies Grow Up to Be Cowboys • My Heroes Have Always Been Cowboys • Stand by Me • Save the Last Dance for Me • You're the First Time I've Thought About Leaving • You're the Reason God Made Oklahoma • many more.

00360730......................$15.95

Hot Country Dancin'

Over 30 toe-tapping, boot-scootin' favorites guaranteed to get you dancing! Includes: Achy Breaky Heart • Friends in Low Places • Here's a Quarter (Call Someone Who Cares) • Hey, Good Lookin' • I Feel Lucky • and more.

00311621......................$12.95

The Award-Winning Songs of the Country Music Association – 1984-1996

40 country award-winners, including: Achy Breaky Heart • Ain't That Lonely Yet • Baby's Got Her Blue Jeans On • Boot Scootin' Boogie • Daddy's Hands • Down at the Twist and Shout • Forever and Ever, Amen • Friends in Low Places • God Bless the U.S.A. • I Swear • The Keeper of the Stars • Where've You Been • and more. Also includes a photo library of the winners.

00313081......................$17.95

Contemporary Country

Features 49 hot country hits: Amazed • Blue • A Broken Wing • Cowboy Take Me Away • He Didn't Have to Be • I Love You • I'm Alright • Little Red Rodeo • Longneck Bottle • Ready to Run • Single White Female • many more!

00310587......................$17.95

Country Love

27 songs of down-home lovin': The Battle Hymn of Love • Check Yes or No • Could I Have This Dance • Grow Old With Me • The Keeper of the Stars • Let's Go to Vegas • More Than You'll Ever Know • She Is His Only Need • You Decorated My Life • You're Still the One • and more.

00310516......................$14.95

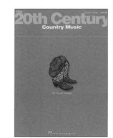

20th Century Country Music

Over 70 country classics representative of a century's worth of music, including: All the Gold in California • Always on My Mind • Amazed • Blue Moon of Kentucky • Boot Scootin' Boogie • Breathe • Crazy • Friends in Low Places • Harper Valley P.T.A. • Hey, Good Lookin' • Ring of Fire • and more.

00310673......................$19.95

Country Inspiration – 2nd Edition

23 sentimental favorites, including: Brotherly Love • I Saw the Light • Love Can Build a Bridge • Love Without End, Amen • The Vows Go Unbroken • Why Me Lord? • and more.

00311616......................$10.95

Good Ol' Country

58 old-time favorites: Candy Kisses • Cold, Cold Heart • Crazy • Crying in the Chapel • Deep in the Heart of Texas • Faded Love • Green Green Grass of Home • Hey, Good Lookin' • I Can't Stop Loving You • Sweet Dreams • Tennessee Waltz • You Are My Sunshine • You Don't Know Me • more.

00310517......................$14.95

The Best Contemporary Country Ballads

30 heart-felt hits, including: After All This Time • Alibis • The Greatest Man I Never Knew • I Can Love You like That • I Meant Every Word He Said • I Want to Be Loved like That • If Tomorrow Never Comes • One Boy, One Girl • When You Say Nothing at All • Where've You Been • more.

00310116......................$14.95

Today's Women of Country

Includes 24 hits by top artists such as LeAnn Rimes, Reba McEntire, Faith Hill, Pam Tillis, Trisha Yearwood and others. Songs include: Blue • Down at the Twist and Shout • The Greatest Man I Never Knew • I Feel Lucky • Mi Vida Loca (My Crazy Life) • When You Say Nothing at All • more!

00310446......................$12.95